more Eclectic Owls

a
coloring
book
for
adults

Eclectic Coloring Books Vol. 5

More Eclectic Owls
Eclectic Coloring Books Vol. 5

Streetlight Graphics Publishing
For information on other books in the *Eclectic Coloring Book* Series please visit: www.StreetlightGraphicsPublishing.com

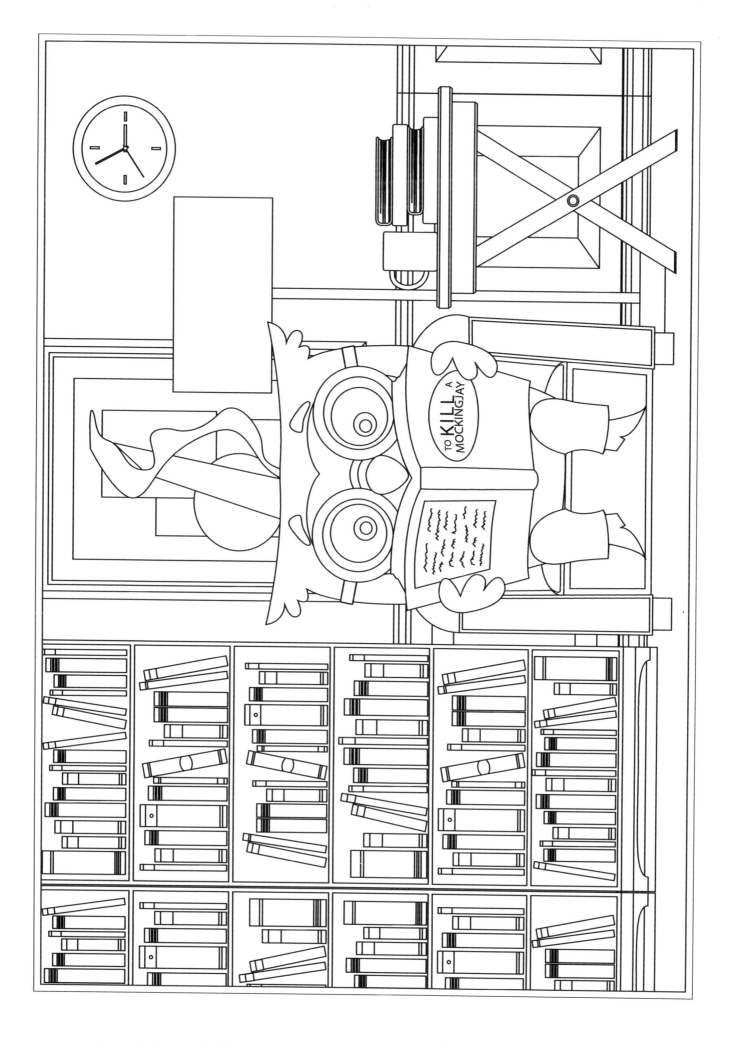

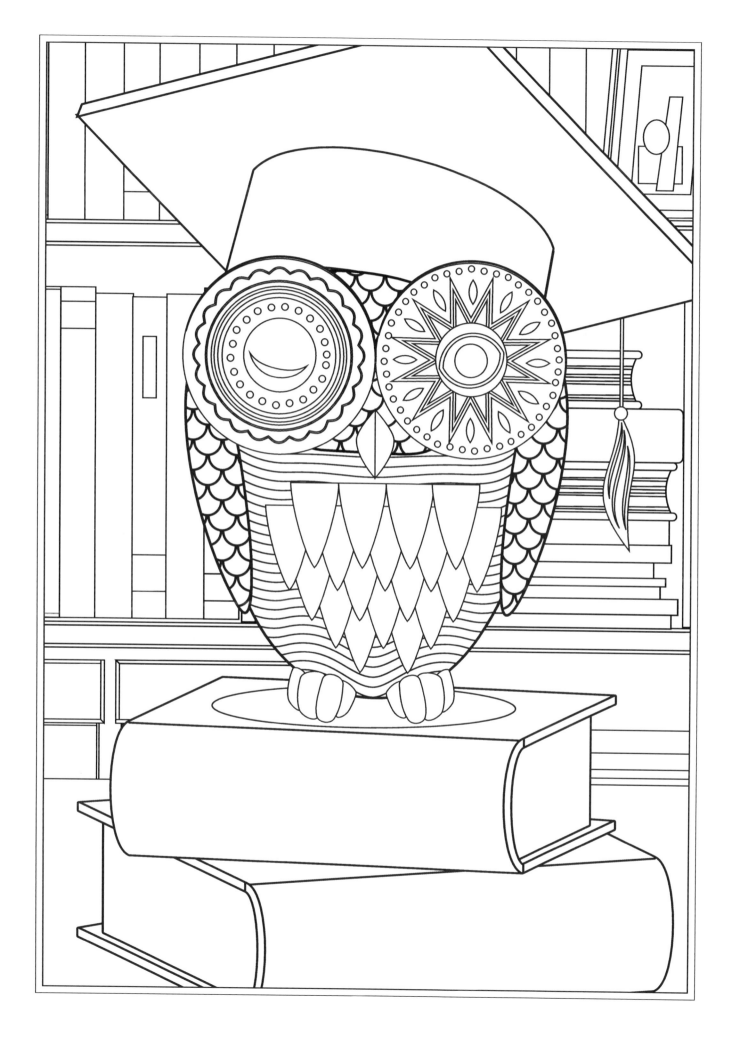

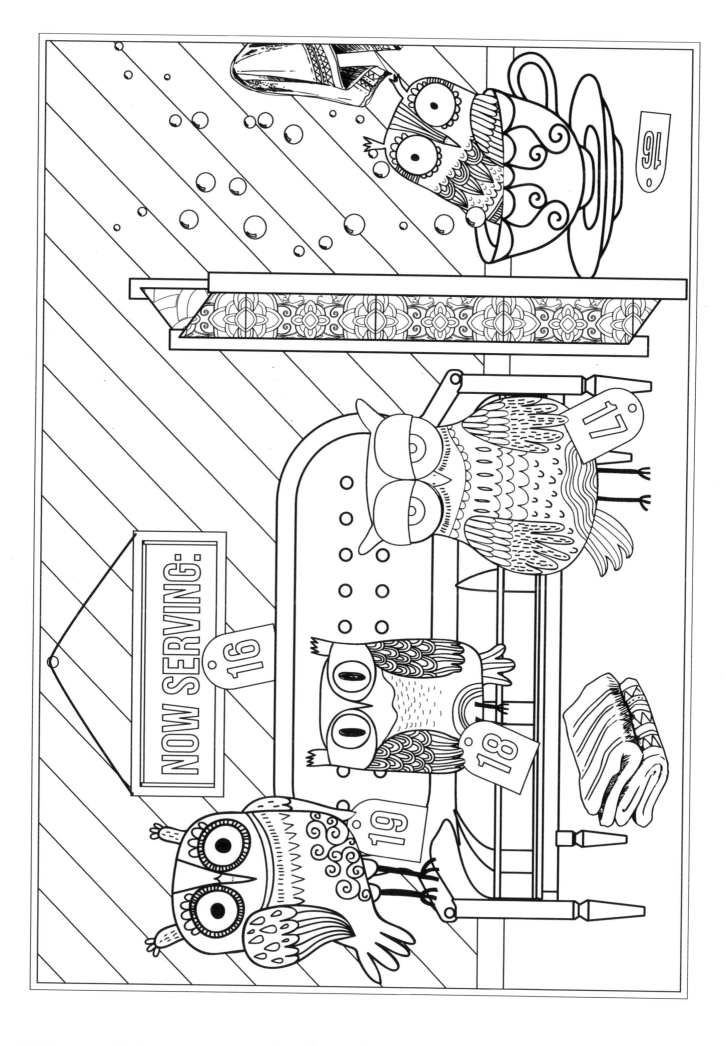

Use this page to test your colors and check for bleed.

Notes and Stuff

Coloring Chart

COLOR	DESCRIPTION		COLOR	DESCRIPTION

Use this handy chart to test your colors and keep track of their names. Simply apply some color into the color column and then label them with the marker, pencil, or crayon color name. This way you will know exactly how that color will look on the page.

Coloring Chart

COLOR	DESCRIPTION		COLOR	DESCRIPTION

Use this handy chart to test your colors and keep track of their names. Simply apply some color into the color column and then label them with the marker, pencil, or crayon color name. This way you will know exactly how that color will look on the page.

Coloring Chart

COLOR	DESCRIPTION		COLOR	DESCRIPTION

Use this handy chart to test your colors and keep track of their names. Simply apply some color into the color column and then label them with the marker, pencil, or crayon color name. This way you will know exactly how that color will look on the page.

Coloring Chart

COLOR	DESCRIPTION		COLOR	DESCRIPTION

Use this handy chart to test your colors and keep track of their names. Simply apply some color into the color column and then label them with the marker, pencil, or crayon color name. This way you will know exactly how that color will look on the page.